SONGS FOR TWO CHILDREN

On Dissociation
And Human Energy Fields

Colin A. Ross, M.D.

Manitou Communications, Inc.

Copyright © 2004 Manitou Communications, Inc.
1701 Gateway, Suite 349
Richardson, TX 75080
Phone: 1-800-572-9588, FAX: 972-918-9069

www.manitoucommunications.com
www.rossinst.com
rossinst@rossinst.com

Designed by Deep River Design
www.deepriverdesign.com

Printed in Canada

ISBN: 0-9704525-9-4

Library of Congress Catalog Number: 2004105954

Colin A. Ross

Songs For Two Children: On Dissociation And Human Energy Fields

1. Poetry   2. Psychiatry   3. Dissociation

ISBN: 0-9704525-9-4

BY THE AUTHOR

Northern Studies (1975)

Portrait Of Norman Wells (1979)

Adenocarcinoma And Other Poems (1984)

Multiple Personality Disorder:
Diagnosis, Clinical Features, And Treatment (1989)

The Osiris Complex:
Case Studies In Multiple Personality Disorder (1994)

Satanic Ritual Abuse: Principles Of Treatment (1995)

Pseudoscience In Biological Psychiatry (1995)

Dissociative Identity Disorder:
Diagnosis, Clinical Features, And Treatment Of Multiple Personality,
Second Edition (1997)

The Trauma Model:
A Solution To The Problem Of Comorbidity In Psychiatry (2000)

BLUEBIRD:
Deliberate Creation Of Multiple Personality By Psychiatrists (2000)

Spirit Power Drawings:
The Foundation Of A New Science (2004)

Schizophrenia: Innovations in Diagnosis and Treatment (2004)

The Great Psychiatry Scam:
One Shrink's Personal Journey (in press)

The Rape Of Eve:
The True Story Behind The Three Faces Of Eve (in press)

CONTENTS

INTRODUCTION

Simeon Leavis Ross,
Born April 29, 1973, Inuvik, Northwest Territories, Canada

Dana Ceridwen Ross,
Born June 7, 1975, Inuvik, Northwest Territories, Canada

My two children, Dana and Simeon, are three-eighths native North American. Their maternal grandmother was a full-blooded Slavey Indian and their maternal grandfather is half-blood Chippewyan. I am pure white, of Celtic ancestry. Today, Dana was notified that she was accepted to begin medical school at the University of Calgary in the fall. Simeon is four days away from Quebec on his walk across Canada to raise money for cancer research. Simeon has released several independent CDs as a solo singer and as lead singer and guitarist for an alternative rock band.

I am a psychiatrist specializing in psychological trauma and dissociation. In 1981, I received my M.D. from the University of Alberta in Edmonton, then completed my psychiatry training at the University of Manitoba in Winnipeg in 1985. Ever since moving to Dallas, Texas in 1991, I have been running a hospital-based Trauma Program. I wrote *Songs For Two Children* in order to explain to my two children my philosophy, my love for them, and my pride in them.

Songs For Two Children is written in iambic pentameter couplets. It is my first long poem. There are several technical devices I want to point out, since some readers may not be aware of them without guidance. First, the basic rhythm is a strong iambic pentameter reminiscent of the English poet Ben Johnson. Pentameter means that there are ten syllables in each line (five sets of two syllables, hence the penta in pentameter), and iambic means the stress is on the even-numbered syllables. Couplets means that the lines rhyme in pairs. The predominant style of *Songs For Two Children* is a plain style, but some passages are in a more ornate style. Ornate and plain are the two basic classical styles of English poetry.

Quiet often, passages are written in sprung rhythm, which was developed by the English poet, Gerard Manley Hopkins. This rhythm is found most beautifully written in poems of his like *The Windhover* and *God's Grandeur*.

In iambic pentameter, the stress is a strong, regular stress on every second syllable. An example is the couplet in lines 37 and 38 of *Songs For Two Children*:

> I said that word before and say again
> I seek a knowledge lost to modern men.

Hopkins named his rhythm *sprung rhythm* because it seems to contain a spring in it. When the rhythm is sprung, the accent may be on the odd syllables in the line and two, or even three or four, syllables in a row may be stressed. One word in the line feels like it has sprung out of the preceding one rhythmically. This effect can be striking at the end of a line, as in some lines by the English poet, John Donne.

Combined with sprung rhythm is another device developed most fully in Hopkins, but also used by Shakespeare, Donne, Eliot and Blake. In this technique, the words rhythmically enact their meaning – they actually do what they say. For instance, John Donne writes, in his *Satyre III*:

> On a huge hill,
> Cragged, and steep, Truth stands, and hee that will
> Reach her, about must, and about must goe;
> And what the hills suddenness resists, winne so.

In these lines the rhythm climbs the hill, stands on a precipice at the end of the first line, and then becomes cragged and steep before it stands firmly planted in the words, 'Truth stands.' The rhythm stretches and reaches out into space at the end of the second line, and then its fist grabs shut with the words, 'Reach her.' Next the rhythm goes and goes about in the second half of the line; it finishes by moving off into space again with the word 'goe.' Then the rhythm brakes itself in the word 'suddenness' and develops strong resistance by the time it gets to the word 'resists.' This muscular quality of language occurs only in poetry and only in poetry do the words rhythmically enact their meaning. An example from *Songs For Two Children* is lines 120-124:

> Deep buried modern man can't think or feel.
> He thinks dead thoughts and European things
> At dusk a dull bell tolls and steeple rings
> A tale of time run out: his foot is shod,
> I said, with iron, as is his soul, not God.

The tolling motion of the bell and its ringing sound are enacted in the third line, and there is a pause at the end of line 122 while the bell rings, due to the rhyme with 'things.' The rhythm runs out and stops by the word 'out' in line 123, but then has become solid and firm again by the word 'iron.' The rhythm in line 124 begins with iambic pentameter and then is sprung, and the vocabulary echoes Hopkins. For instance, 'as is his soul' involves four stressed syllables in a row, a pause created by the comma, then two more stressed syllables at the end of the line.

Sprung rhythm is created by use of assonance and alliteration, and by rhymes and near-rhymes occurring within lines. There can also be rhymes and near-rhymes between words at the ends of lines and words in the interior of preceding and succeeding lines. As well, sprung rhythm is created by variations on vowel sounds within a short space, coupled with variations in the distance between a repeated vowel sound and a repeated consonant. These devices occur throughout *Songs For Two Children*.

Another technical innovation is a series of lines in which a phrase both completes the preceding meaning and initiates the following meaning. The effect is one of overlapping short sentences tied together to become one long sentence. In such passages, the rhythm may also enact the meaning of the line. An example is lines 158-163:

> Not knowing how to heal, how to repair
> His mind. Structure within structure without
> Mirrors itself. Within the mind and out
> Man built a wall to trap himself within
> His concrete earth without is mirrored in
> His mind.

I have described some of the technical aspects of the poem because not many twenty-first century readers are familiar with these aspects of poetry. Being aware of the rhythmical devices may help the reader to hear them with his or her inner ear. In reading poetry, it is essential to read out loud inside your head and at the correct speed. It is impossible to speed-read poetry and really read the rhythms, just like it is impossible to hear the reality of a piece of music if it is played faster than it should be on a CD player. In order to 'hear' the music, it has to be played at the right speed.

I learned about the rhythmical and technical properties of English poetry by reading the works of the English literary critic, F.R. Leavis, especially his two books, *New Bearings in English Poetry* and *Revaluation.* I agree with his evaluation of T.S. Eliot, and my favorite Eliot poems are *A Song For Simeon*, *Marina* and *Four Quartets.* The opening lines of *A Song For Simeon* enact their meaning rhythmically, as Leavis pointed out. However, in Eliot, unlike in Donne, the muscles of the rhythm are weak, light and barely alive; these rhythms enact and communicate the spiritual condition of their author, which is also communicated by the meaning of his words. Eliot wrote:

> Lord, the Roman hyacinths are blooming in bowls and
> The winter sun creeps by the snow hills;
> The stubborn season has made stand.
> My life is light, waiting for the death wind,
> Like a feather on the back of my hand.
> Dust in sunlight and memories in corners
> Wait for the wind that chills towards the dead land.

As in Donne, the rhythm enacts the 'standing' action of the word 'stand,' but Eliot's spiritual feet are much less firm, less muscular, and less planted. Likewise, his flowers are blooming in bowls, not in the earth. The rhythm of the second line creeps along till it pauses after the word 'by,' before visual attention shifts to the hills. The rhythm of the last line is faulting and hesitant, and it runs down an energy slope as if towards death. These themes of artificiality, death, disintegration, lack of roots and the failure of natural, sensual life predominate in other Eliot poems such as *Gerontion*, *The Love Song of J. Alfred Prufrock* and *The Wasteland.*

In poetry, the actual quality of experience can be communicated with a precision not approached by any other means, as Leavis said. The words communicate not just through meaning, but through rhythm and sound. They have color and tension. Poetry creates a muscular tension within words and in the spaces between words, much like the tensions in space created by a Henry Moore sculpture. The goal is for the technical devices to be inseparable from the poetry's meaning, and vice versa. Thought, feeling, perception, arousal level, and internal psychological tension are all communicated simultaneously and recreated in the internal space of the reader as he or she reads.

A few of the references in *Songs For Two Children* may be obscure to readers who have not studied English poetry, but they are not hard to understand. For instance 'Red Hanrahan' is a figure in poems by W.B. Yeats, which also include references to gongs and the 'gong-tormented sea.' Whenever I mention Yeats, I usually echo rhythm and vocabulary from poems of his like *Byzantium, Sailing To Byzantium* and *Among School Children*. In one of his poems, John Donne puns on his name and the word 'done,' while talking about God, and I echo that in my poem. These echoes are my way of paying homage to my teachers. I have included a few notes at the end of the poems to clarify other references.

Songs For Two Children was written in hotel rooms in Los Angeles, Beijing, China, Melbourne, Australia and Loch Lomond, Scotland. As well, lines were written in airplanes over the Pacific and Atlantic oceans, and over the continental United States. The remaining lines were composed in my office in Richardson, Texas.

Colin A. Ross, M.D.
Santa Barbara, California
May 9, 2004

THE
SONGS

A Song
For Simeon

Tight rhythm and rhyme can tell in time tales
In sinew, muscle, bone. Prose alone fails
Therefore I write in rhyme to tell you this –
The road to God is not a path of bliss.
No pain no gain. Required: hard discipline.
I tell that truth in age, not youth; my spleen
Is gone, my teeth, my knees, but not my tongue.
It Deus deemed should live – forever young?

Not that but time to talk to rhyme in thought
A story of a war not won but fought   10
On battlefields of mind. Lord, not to lose
Is the one outcome I would ever choose
And I do, Lord, in your name and your grace
For the future and for the human race.

The land was burned, trees bared, mothers buried
In the dead earth – a bomb by plane carried
Killed more, one day, than any axe could hew
And brought an end to war. I ask, then, you –
Trees died in an instant and a bright cloud
Einstein manufactured but who allowed?   20

What, Lord, is life? Old gods, blind fate, mere chance?
The product of a subatomic dance?
Or cold nothing, whirling atoms, a void
Perhaps ants stepped on by bored gods annoyed
By them? I pose this problem with my pen

Till now not answered by women or men.
I listen for your lesson, Lord, but hear
No meaning in man, in Homer or Lear,
Great works but not of this millennium.
Newer knowledge forged in titanium   30
Would better suit this age and so I seek
For it in valley and on mountain peak
In the one mind I know, my own, my Lord,
And so to you I dedicate my sword
Mightier than most pens and yet too weak
To find I fear the answers that I seek.

I said that word before and say again
I seek a knowledge lost to modern men.
Old gods and freedoms, and a source of life
Severed once by an ancient mental knife   40
Called human reason or else intellect.
Doctor of history, I now dissect
The past to find the future so I go
Where solitude takes me, go high and low
In a labyrinthine lair man has made
To hide, far from the field where life is played.

Mere merriment of maids, moonlight and dew
Were themes before which Shelley thought would do.
They now do not. The moon shines still and stars
Do too but men can't touch them, not in cars   50
Or trucks or trains because their brains, their minds
Are shut, no if and or but, behind blinds
Man made, nor can foot feel, being shod – God
As Hopkins held, because the mind is flawed
Cannot be felt not in this world, not now.

I endeavor to write not why, but how
A psychiatric treatise for the West.
Until that's done the mind can't sleep can't rest.
Restless worried anxious women know too
We need not pills but water, clear and true.

60

An analytical test showed man is
Devoid of mass and weight, mere gas, like fizz
I used to make with tablets in my youth
To drink at lunch: Lord, I was then uncouth.

Modern man makes much patriotic noise
He flaunts his guns and planes and boats and toys
Which protect him: he wonders why the hate
Of foreign fools has found his soil, of late.

School shooters and gang thugs have told the tale
With acts of condemnation but they pale   70
Beside the shots he's fired. He fears the Lord
Still but is willing to unsheath his sword
In any battle: 'defend the nation'
For him requires no justification.

Man medicates his brain but not his soul
Which does not work. There is, I fear, a hole
That can't be filled in it. Though one might think
That, a grim diagnosis made in ink,
There is hope here to heal the hurting mind
In me. If not, the death of human kind   80
Is near, or done and that cannot be borne
By me, my Lord, therefore duty to warn
Kicks in. I think these things that you, my Sim,

Will walk a road that does not lead to him,
That modern man I call Neanderthal
As Arthur Koestler did, if I recall
Darkness At Noon quite right: I think I do
And so I dedicate this poem to you
First son, your life begun my only child
Followed by four, born in the northern wild.   90

Old ancestors gave you an ancient sense
Of life of God in a cold land, immense
And strong. I saw into your eyes one time
At two months old: remember this in rhyme;
I saw that wild no white man knew but me
In Norman Wells, in you. That's how I see
You now, covered with white man sweat and smell
Stuck in lower levels of white man's Hell
And yet not lost because your blood is strong
And from it comes a creed, a life, a song   100
That is alive. Sim, modern man is dead
He walks upon not earth but Hell instead
He made himself, with concrete, glass and steel.

Ten moons have set since his last breath and meal
Or no, ten long decades, or more – his soul
Sleeps now silent lost in a sad deep hole
Dark, dead or dull. I cannot tell which way
His soul is now. There may not be a day
When it awakes – till then, his fate, my son
I hope will not be thine. My Lord, your sun   110
Shine on him his life his children, wife, friends
His thoughts, song, body, mind; his life depends
On you, your grace, your light, your touch. His race

Is partly white, but he has blood. With grace
He has a chance: knowledge locked in his genes
Might make him free. I see what such thought means:
He got his genes from me. Locked down longer
In white people they might be pale, stronger
Or dead, underneath concrete, glass and steel.

Deep buried modern man can't think or feel.   120
He thinks dead thoughts and European things
At dusk a dull bell tolls and steeple rings
A tale of time run out: his foot is shod,
I said, with iron, as is his soul, not God.

Man walks within walls in a world he built
Based on anger, on sin, and shame and guilt.

And man's false God, Jesus, once among us
Is remembered here with fanfare and fuss
In human form each Sunday morning. Lord
I mean your Son whose side and soul were gored   130
By man. He walks not on earth now. A ghost
Inhabits modern man who is his host:
'I have Jesus in my heart.' At the end
Of time an empty Jesus is man's friend.

Therefore I could turn to teepees and drums
But no, I'm white – when I am right what comes
To me's the wind that makes trees sing. Their sound
Calls 'Colin come to me.' Therein I found
A hole leading to an old world or time
I send you in ten syllables and rhyme.   140

A god is there, Sim, at Jessica Lake
And Canyon Creek. It was man's worst mistake
To stop that hole with doubt, false ritual
And intellect which caused the burial
Of God. I study minds that broke and split
In two caused by trauma – just so much shit
Can be borne by children. My race has got
That sickness too split from itself in thought
And in feeling: dissociated mind,
The psychiatric ill of human kind.   150

Man's split from God, woman, child and nature
And has become God's lowliest creature.
Man tries to kill the things he loves. His thirst
For death cannot be slaked. Therefore, at first,
Treatment won't work. He has to see the light.
Till then man moves in an endless dark night
Of black blindness, deafness, and of despair,
Not knowing how to heal, how to repair
His mind. Structure within structure without
Mirrors itself. Within the mind and out   160
Man built a wall to trap himself within
His concrete earth without is mirrored in
His mind. He buried our Mother Earth God
And won't touch her. Likewise, man's mind is flawed –
He buried God within so can't know Him
(A diagnosis of death I've made, Sim)
Or his own self, the source of life and song
Sung once by Yeats' tormented gyre and gong
Which rang dead time, sang metronome rhythm.

There is a rhyme that could be mine: vision's   170

Required; it all revolves on what one makes
With words, what living turns, what stops and breaks
At a line's end. A figure skater's curse
Is this, to turn and then to turn, or worse
Again, to fall on the hard ice, not once
Twice, but a dozen times. But Sim, for once
My news is good. Sim, contemplate my ruse:
My Ross trick jump works well. I get no bruise
If my rhyme's wrong, or song. Paper and pen
Are my ice rink. When this shrink falls down then   180
He's not sick. Words have done the trick. The jump's
In space in mind and he receives no bumps.

So, Sim, my work's in mind instead. Our race,
Yours, hers, and mine is dying in this place
No air to breathe nor earth to touch, within
And, too, without. The white man's mortal sin
Is that he built a barrier in mind
As in the world. My work is then to find
A hole to join the earth and sky so light
Can come down here so that the earth just might   190
Bloom its dark bulbs that then become flowers
A pagan vision of earth's dark powers
From which Jesus was born. Man's mind has banned
The Earth and made Her dead, covered the land
With lies, highways and dissociation
Thereby burying many a nation.

The first step, Sim, is history taking
Then diagnosis is in the making.
I dedicate these steps to you, my son,
And pray, one day God's will on earth be done.   200

A Song For Dana

To make her grade a girl will work will read
Will learn to not love live or be in need.
Dear Dana Do you cannot play a fool
If your life goal is a medical school.

I've walked that route, the road to Dr. Ross
I know the work, the grind – the mind, the loss
It lives is real. Brain cells sure shut down, smells
Aren't smelled, trips not taken, in living Hells
We call college courses. Oh well, the end
Justifies the means: that lie will well bend   210
The truth for you. There's nothing else to do
Therefore I am a well wisher for you.

I wish the well does yield its earned reward
When all your tests are normed when you have scored
Quite high enough on the MCAT. Your grades
Are good your zeal is great, no study aids
Will get you there, just you. I know, I've learned
As you learn now lessons that are long burned
In my old brain. There's little to explain
To you because all doctors learn of pain   220
In life not just from books, at least I did.

Today these lessons are not dead or hid
From you. They're told in rhyme, and deed, in word
And by action with pen, not by the sword.
My war is fought on fields where flowers wilt

Without water and without life: my kilt
Tartan and brogue are dead: no bagpipe plays
For them: all that history, those nights and days
Of yore are gone, here on this concrete plain
That knows no God, no gourd of life, no rain,   230
Only a dull light bulb that shines at night
And with its magic makes a kind of sight
That sees no God, only, Dana, a room
In which a knight lies sleeping; I presume
It's Corpus Christi, or, a long dead god
Of a mid-Eastern sect we've now outlawed
Since terrorists flew planes one fateful day –
Nine eleven to be precise. I'd say
Two worlds crashed then and that the flames that burst
Forth then have been well fanned since then. The worst   240
Is yet to be, to live in this new world
Of hate, not of healing. Old flags unfurled
And flown from poles proclaim the hate of men
Once buried, and resurrected again
Buried and then reborn in cycles. Why
That is, I know not, Dana. In the sky
The answer lives but not here on this earth
We have not given it name, form or birth
Nor will we now or soon. Given these facts
Healing still counts. It is one of man's acts   250
That is still good, still God driven, God made
Us for such work although his Son was laid
To rest by hate, he still moves here – his heart
Still beats in this thorax, he is a part
Of me and thee, Dana. He's not enough
However; I need more than Jesus tough
Though that is to know true though it is. Yes

There is more truth to life, unless my guess
Is wrong, Dana. An older knowledge, lost
By modern man who has incurred great cost 260
As a result. Rooted in Mother Earth
A plant can breed as mankind can, give birth
To progeny of bone and mind, flowers
That love that live from their dark roots their hours
On earth. Physics not faith proclaims this thing
Like Kepler said celestial souls sing
But man is deaf, mute, blind; he cannot hear
That voice. We kept Kepler's facts, but, it's clear,
Not his vision. Physics and faith were once
One. Man once bowed before no graven dunce 270
He called science. Lo, man's new God is dead.

He lives in the dissociated head
Of Godless man, only. I now propose
A new marriage, a partnership of those
Parties parted by Descartes, dualism,
And science: spirit and matter. Schism
Has been man's lot since God died man forgot
His pagan roots older than Sodom, Lot
Adam and Eve, at least so I believe.

Conjoined by God, body and soul could cleave 280
Together, one flesh, one mind. Being so
They could be cured of the disease, the slow
Virus infecting them since the day God
Died, or was banned or martyred, or outlawed
Or cast into a Hell of disbelief
From which the scientific soul's relief
Has yet to come. My theory says that mind

Is made from matter, and that humankind
Is but one place it is. Others are rock,
Wind, tree, and lake. The root, the branch, the stalk   290
And the blossom come from a common seed
According to my theory, to my creed.
Spirit is a property of matter.

The claptrap rumor mill mindless chatter
Of caged monkeys, men, hid the roots of mind
Old yogis placed in heart, gut, throat; you'll find
Them there I think. An EEG can tell
I'm right, at least as I predict. Farewell
Dead text, and welcome new religion. Hell

Can bloom, Hades, whatever name we spell.   300
Dark gut plexes give life. I know this well.

I've drawn my learning, Lord, from the dark well
Of my own mind; it is not faith, I say,
It's science. Experiments will prove one day
Plexus readings can differentiate
Mania, gloom, an anxious mental state
Or Alzheimer's, from psychotic soul loss.
The physiology of Colin Ross
Permits studies Newton did not conduct.

He lacked theory, vision and the product   310
Of many men's hard work. A technical
Advance married to theoretical
Thinking makes strides one leg could not. The march
Of knowledge needs two legs. A sunken arch
Arthritic heel and a bad hip are man's

Condition now. My theory involves plans
To fix the lower limbs of man. A gut
Feeling is fact not superstition but
We have no proof as yet, therefore my lab
Will seek it. A preliminary stab   320
Is this: fright scripts provoke a solar flare
Before cognition starts to think, to care.

The facts go in; they then are sent two ways,
First down, then up. Here, this is how it plays
In my belief: a signal to the gut
Provokes responses we all know but shut
Out from science. An EEG can track
Events like that. Theory opens the crack.

By testing chakras, turning them to fact
Old knowledge gets new clothes and the impact   330
Has a broad scope – yes, a paradigm shift
Occurred to me and I make it my gift
To you, your world and your future, thereby
Building connection between Earth and Sky
Body and mind. D.H. Lawrence wrote down
His guiding words for me but now I own
My own version, doctor for mind and heart,
Advocate for science, and too, for art.

Subjective truth that man locked out breaks back
In. Doors are cracked open and my attack   340
Does not falter. Mind rooted in body
Is a hypothesis I will study
Not just believe. Energy fields in man
And without man, between man and rock can

Be studied now and meters can be built
To capture them. The segments of my quilt
Need more stitching before the work is done
Like Donne my work is not done but begun
First by God, done by Him, through me, then me
I bring it out, or up, or down, to see   350
It bear fruit here on Earth. Get a reading
Of Sedona rock – Dana, my meaning
Is this: there is dysynchrony in us
In modern man, in the solar plexus
That can be measured, can be cured I think
By mystic meditation by a shrink
Focused on rock energy, tuned to it:
Between that man and rock a better fit
Results. I've done this work in my own mind   360
A way to make music, celestial
Science, and then rise above bestial
Brutal strata of evolution, rise
Up to science, not rest in mere surmise.

Shamanic tricks worked well, but how, and why?
They brought fertility to Earth and Sky.
Well focused fields of thought, of mind, could make
Seeds germinate, of this make no mistake.

Meters could measure it could give the mode
The median of mind, a mother lode   370
For venture capital. I'll build a switch
Activated by eyebeam and that stitch
Will make my quilt complete. I'll have the proof:
Men don't debate a demonstrated truth

Which is religion too. Those two are one
Or will be if my mortal work is done.

When I am done the work will have begun
Will not be done, it will live like John Donne
But when I'm done, 'twill be not Donne but me
Who will have done the work, and so, you see   380
The mortal mind can touch a tree, a rock,
The wind, ticking to an old ancient clock
And change its charge, its field, or change itself
To be more attuned to rock, God and self:
Immanent realism. What star mind song
Did Kepler sing, what music or what gong
Did he play, long ago? The beat, the tune
Were hidden in a rhyme, by Yeats, a rune
Or some old barn Red Hanrahan had found

Tormented by a silent song, a sound   390
His mind could hear. Old hints, old haunts, I know
Them well but Yeats knew not the way to go
My own pathway I find I walk thereby
In touch with the Keplerian night sky
Night gods, night vision too. Dana, the sun
Shines bright on Hanrahan and on my one
Vision. No moonlit night will win the war
On spiritual death, even the score
Or right the wrong Descartes enshrined: God mind
In matter is the spring I strive to find.   400

A SECOND
SONG
FOR SIMEON

He told the truth with word and deed. His death
Gave man real hope, real life and even breath
In this world in the next but now Jesus
Sleeps in dead Bibles. He here among us
Walks not and no water springs from his rock
Which is, which was and which will be. Christ's clock
No longer ticks, time's standing still. Einstein
Said God does not play dice with worlds. That's fine
But God now plays nothing. How nice. His harp
Is still, his heart can't beat, a sudden sharp   410
Pain's felt by man, a cardiac arrest
Has taken hold of him therefore the best
He does is twitches, gags or shots from guns
From foxholes under harsh Iraqi suns.

Dead man asks why mad Muslim men attack
His corpse the West. I need an open crack
It's all I ask for – air. Sing a prayer
Sim, for Allah since man will not, nor care.
Is Allah dead? He is, in Western man
And lives elsewhere. Sim, sing that if you can.   420
The crack has several shapes. It's in the mind
Potential air, life, light for human kind.

That walk you plan to take is one, your song
And laugh, tears shed for Grandma who lived long
In her cold North who lies in Norman Wells
Under earth, held closely by soothing swells

Of a heaving ocean drifting through time
God's hand lifting up her soul said your rhyme
As mine does too. She took hard knocks at school.
A graduate of life she was a tool –   430
Indian mind. Cecelia knew the North
And she does still. I feel that she brought forth
A knowledge, Sim, we've lost in our dead world.

She dreams her ancient dreams. Her soul lies curled
In God's great lap. It always did, pagan,
Female, her heart beat to an Indian
Rhythm, old truth, spirit, to tobacco
The river took from her. She gave it so
River gods would know. But what touch, you ask,
Was that? The hand of man, which was her task.   440
She did it well, and touched me too. I've met
No wiser woman here, on earth, not yet.

Old warriors walk the woods. No winter lair
Holds them, those ghosts of lives long lived, it's fair
To say, ago. Their shining robes have been
Atop the mountain, Sim, where no machine
Can walk, and Sun dips down but does not set.

Great medicine that mountain top could get
For man, if he would go. But he does not
So modern knowledge is his lot; man's got   450
Nothing. A metal plate within his neck
Has made body and man's mind disconnect –
Nature versus nurture, man against beast
While Satan wars with God, and in the East
No sun rises. Dark realms rule here and no

Stars shine. A mind map might help us, although
It's just a start. We know the truth but shut
It out, therefore my thought: we need the gut
And head to talk. Data our ganglia
Receive get blocked by our amnesia   460
For the old source, of life and of knowledge
That Cecelia knew. Sim, men allege
Dumb tribes believed in a discarnate life
Source then call them superstitious. My knife
Can kill that speech, my pen, which is my sword
As I have said. Man's thoughts block out the Lord.

Gut feelings give us facts. We gather good
Smoke signals through them too, or so we should.
Solar plexes, says Dr. Ross, can read
The world like radio phones do. We need   470
To listen, Sim. Data come through those ports
Once called chakras. We cancel all reports
Before our brains get them. A plate blocks out
The sound so, Sim, man's deaf and that's about
The end of it. Technology could track
These facts if man allowed a little crack
To creep into his mind and his world view.

There's nothing more that modern man can do
To save his soul; it too is locked beneath
The plate. Blue Druids dancing on a heath   480
Might help man heal, but I think not: their time
On earth is done. Yet, Celtic rhythm, rhyme
And blood flow still in arteries that write
And tell the tale as any man's mind might
If he knew God. I mean my own. What tale,

You ask? Born blue barely breathing a pale
Baby of the white race, I dream I fly,
A latter day shaman, from Earth to Sky
But wake. Another road might work, but which?

What myth can meet man's need? The poor, the rich,   490
The same thirst they suffer and the dead dust
From which they came is where they live; men must,
It's said, return again and then return
To birth to death each season in its turn
Then turn again the grinding wheel of God
Has got the soul held tight and a crow cawed
To mark it's dawn. Which men were there? I was
And you were too. We walked the cliff because
It was our lot who overlook the brink
Of Hell. We have more truth to seek, I think.   500

A SECOND
SONG
FOR DANA

Dana, a demon can't know God. They hate
All things God made, yet Satan is God's mate
Or, His mirror, made by God, given life
By Him: His Evil Bride is God's Good Wife
Or so a monk once wrote, or Celtic bard
Or else wizard. That truth when told is hard
To hear: most men do not, in robe or gown,
Or know that an angel once fell far down
To Earth, rebel against his God. A dearth
Of real freedom galled him. He rules the Earth   510
Now and has and he will unless the rage
A few good men can feel can heal the Age.

Anger at God is bad, man says, but he
Follows Satan to sin to death, you see,
Therefore man's love is clear: he feels no fear
Before Mary, Jesus or God. I hear
His death rattle on my TV. The rule
Of dark Satan is seed, or is a tool
To break the cage of man. The morning star
Is Lucifer who fell from God fell far   520
In pride in lust seeking justice: God's wife
Left Him but he is married still in life
And death, to Him, is Him, His own project
Called back by me who's felt too much neglect
By God. Their union is quite good, I'd say,
For man, in man, of man and any day
Now they will be wedded as One by each

Other as once the Bible's words did teach
Which we forgot on Earth. Remember now,
Dana, that truth: black Satan told God how   530
To make him too as all things did. Their Word
Was what God knew or thought or felt or heard –
The Big Bang man now calls the birth of God.

Great pun, great theory too, Dana. The sod
Must now be laid, the corpse covered with dirt
So man's bad myth stays dead. It's caused much hurt
On Earth. Demons don't live man says but I
Think not. Though demons dance in Hell and die
On the judgment, they either are or not
And if they live, Dana, then they have got   540
To have substance, not steel, not wood, not fire –
An energy signature a higher
Hand, God's, wrote down. To scan that frequency
Would be to sin, says man, indecency,
Evil, an infernal union of state
And church. The two have been divorced of late.

But I say not. Across space a divine
Hand reaches God, in a Chapel. This line
My mind, my soul, writes here: I say the Earth
Was God's creation Satan too. Their birth   550
Was One. Man threw Satan down and that sin
Is now undone. Let the healing begin
In my own mind. Dana, discarnate mind
Exists, or not. One task of human kind
Is how to find a sign of it. Mere thought
Cannot. A gauge, meter or scope has got

To be built but cannot if faith and lab
Cannot catch cannot hail the same damn cab.

Whose rule is that? Why man's, of course. His brain
Made it, his God, his faith, I strive again   560
To hate that God, Dana, whom man has made –
His own image stares back at man. I played
That game quite well but quit, here, now, Dana
And hope to get from Heaven, grace, hannah
Or holy bread, black Satan's loaf of rye
Or wheat, not white man's dough, for he must die
For God to live is my one goal – I'd give
His life for His: with His death man will live.

Terrorists know that truth but with their blast
They martyred man which meant his God was cast   570
In stone. That made things worse. Man hunts Evil
In far places, pounds it on his anvil
In a subterranean forge of his.

Therefore God bless man's military biz
His bucks and bombs. It's that old dance man's God
Knows well. Satan is his partner. He thawed
Hell's flames with contradictory ice then
Froze them then melted Hell's ice candles again
And will do again till man tires of that.
It is a dance man's God and he begat.   580

Life after death: no faith has made it fact
Though science could, but how? The mind can act
To solve the riddle – my paradigm shift
Is here my contribution, here my gift

To you. Have it, Dana, for safe-keeping
Hold it with your heart when I am sleeping
And gone. It trickles down at last to scans
A dream of a machine that's not in man's
Unconscious mind as yet. One cannot build
That gauge till Satan rules man's God's been killed.   590

Till then I wait. All things get split by man
Split the atom, split heart and head, split man
From his woman. Saint or sinner, a whore
Or Madonna, hookers well keep the score
In man's death game. Tough terrorists can play
Games too. They whore they drink until the day
They fly into man's church, his holy shrine
Where man works man worships and man does fine
On money markets. Money changers died
That day, Satan said. They did too, and lied.   600

A Third Song For Simeon

My query is, how like you this, my child?
Modern man does not know God nor the wild
In Him. I have, I do, I will, His will
On Earth be done. I'll heal that human ill
But not with drugs not with scalpel, instead
I mean to mend man's soul, to teach the dead
Who walk in Hell. Teach what, you ask? In rhyme
I'll take man out of mere Newtonian time.   610

Time travel's real though no machines can go
To there with their grinding metal gears so
My mind must, Sim. On Loch Lomond's west shore
I wrote these words where old Scots bones before
My time were buried deep in dampest Earth.

A white swan swam and that scene then gave birth
To true lines, Sim. I sing the Loch, its trees,
A Scots ripple rippling in the breeze frees
The mind – great Scotland did, when a rainbow
Reached Loch Lomond's waters therefore I know   620
My roots, and yours. Sitting near a stone wall
The bright night stars shining, cold, clear, and all
The dead awake, thirty-five years before,
In England, in touch with a truth of yore
I felt the stones; dark their energy, slow
Their time. In the solar chakra I know
Those stones' spirit. My flux is theirs, my time
Theirs too. They walk with God. I hope my rhyme

Can too. Old stones hold a knowledge man's lost
And are attuned. Modern man bears the cost   630
Of that. Sim, I traveled outside the age
Of man. I did not strut on man's dead stage
That night. My knowledge, Sim, could then be taught
To man to cure his soul. This patient's caught
In atheism's trap, or Satan's sack
Which like St. Nick he carries on his back.

Man's modern myth is Santa Claus. What truth
Is taught by him in folklore form to youth?
That adults lie, play tricks, that by good deeds
A child can earn his keep can get his needs   640
Met in his life. The gifts came not from God
(The myth is true; its truth is sick and flawed)
Or His white beard but from a bank: your dad
Made bucks to buy those things and aren't you glad?

No God takes care of man. Man tells a tale
Of that but it's a lie that without fail
You'll learn, my child. Santa Satan will bring
Caesar's bounty in his sack, choirs will sing,
On man's most holy days, but I say this:
Man's road is not a route that ends in bliss.   650

St. Nick's Satan, who was transformed. His lame
Wings folded, Black Peter became his name.
He put bad children in a bag, to Hell
Taken. These myths have all been buried well
By man, whose God is dead. A world outside
Man's world was walked one night I sat beside
Those stones. I tell my faith to thee, my son,

That God's will in our lifetime might be done.
But is that faith? Aye, there's the rub: which path
To take, science or God? To solve that math   660
I calculate they're one. Sim, immanent
Realism can cleave the firmament
Can bring God down here, His energy field,
Can welcome Him, so that man's soul is healed
If that's His plan. Lo, an empirical
Cast of mind could well work that miracle
Which takes God's grace and our effort combined
To cure dissociation in the mind
Of man that keeps God locked out, cast out far
Beyond his world. Man shuns the Morning Star   670
Named Lucifer, shining aspect of God.
I say man's broken mind should be outlawed.

In ancient Greece the malady did start:
Man split his world in two, his mind, his art
And science, his Satan and God. Enough
Damage done now. The love man needs is tough
To take but is healing. The opposite
Magnetic pole is part, so I posit,
Of a unified field, and that's my art
My understanding of the head and heart.   680

The brain maintains a field, magnetic, weak,
Compared to earth, but there. The heart can seek
That field with its magnetic reach: fingers
Of the heart touch the brain which then lingers
The heart to touch, and head and heart thus talk,
Their chatter born within earth's field. No clock
Ticked then or cell phone rang, when dull apes grew

Stood up, made tools, evolved to something new
On earth. Those subtle fields I call the soul.
Hard diamond created in earth from coal   690
Is not more clear than that or real. I'll buy
A magnetometer from some smart guy
To measure soul. That's fact and not fiction
For which I need new words, grammar, diction.

Descartes split the body and soul in two –
Disconnection was all that he could do
For man. Since then, I'd say, it's gotten worse
Man's Cartesian dualistic death curse.

I'll measure it. I'll plot its points. My graph
Will give man cause to pause, to pray not laugh.   700
Heart-head desynchronization destroys
The soul or buries it so that no noise
Is heard from it. Sim, the salamander
Chakra has been well mapped by one Becker,
M. D. His book is good his mind is good
Too, great, I'd say but shunned. Sim, if I could
I'd walk his path. I will, I can, I pray.
His moccasin will well fit my foot say
I, Sim. Know this: it's science, Sim, I seek.

I'll partner with an engineering geek   710
To build Colin's Chakra Meter: DC
Positive current nodes I'll find. You'll see.
I'll self-fund, Sim, my lab unless Bill Gates
Will help. He might, or else Paul Dell. The Fates
Will weave their web, the war will be won, Sim;
Those spinning women work the will of Him.

Professors know the eye emits no beam
Though fools think so. The proof of that, 'twould seem,
Comes from John Locke. Man's physics tells his truth
Refuted here. I learned, Lord, in my youth   720
That mine differs. The brain emits a field
Through skull and bone. An EEG will yield
A wave that proves my point. The eye looks out
Through the orbit. Some day I'll have the clout
To prove the evil eye is real, when shorn
Of superstition, Sim. Let me now warn
The dull skeptic: sheath your sword, fool; grim death
Will reap your soul and your physics, your breath
Will end. For you my physics proves too much.

An EEG electrode feels the touch   730
Of an eyebeam when shielded well. The noise
Of our lit world obscures this beam, annoys
The soul too, Sim. I felt it in the woods
But can't in man's electric neighborhoods.
Hunting rabbits I felt an eye and turned
And shot one dead one day and thereby learned
The eyebeam's real: we all have felt its hand.

Closed minds, closed schools and souls can't understand
This truth but I can speak and in my lab
Will prove it true, at least take my best stab   740
At white man lies, at white man war on God,
(Remember Hopkins said man's foot is shod)
And life. Mother Earth holds our souls. Her lap
Is electromagnetic. She can wrap
Us in her arms and has since we evolved
But man seeks outer space. Man's mind is solved

Here, Sim, in one thousand rhymed lines. Man wants
To leave the earth. He has. The world man haunts
Is shielded well from Earth, his cities, cars,
Factories and phones have made a wall; Mars   750
Is man's promised land. No Mother Earth there
No water, life, Earth field, breathable air.

Man's paradise is Hell. He lives there now.
His Earth is Mars. Full well I know that Thou
And I are one, Mother. My Father Sky
I pledge to Thee to seek the how, the why
Of man's ill mind. He put a thick blanket
Between himself and Thee. Who would thank it
That magnetic straight-jacket curse by man
Made man sanctioned? Why man, of course, whose plan   760
Is death. These facts can be measured. The laws
They follow have a scientific cause.

Dysynchrony of brain and Earth, dear Sim,
In a future that is near and not dim
Can be a fact then can be fixed. My school
Of therapy will be a root, a tool
In God's new growth in His garden. Mark here
The line we've crossed with these rhymed words. All fear
Of failure falls before these facts, or will
If such technology can heal the ill   770
In man's body and mind, the disconnect
'Twixt folk wisdom and modern intellect
Between man's brain and Earth, between man's brain
And solar plexus, Sim. There's much to gain
From such science, and much to lose if man
Succeeds in his death game and if his plan

Prevails. Those English stones taught me that time
Moves slow for them. I saw the stars in time
Not mine but theirs: my gut plexus took root
In them, a current flowed from them; the fruit   780
Of it was my vision, my mind. I saw
What they cannot, sightless, but do, made raw
Contact with God, and felt the Earth's great soul
Her electromagnetic field, a whole
Circuit complete. Cold air, cold ground, warm flesh
The stars and earth, all these did touch, did mesh
In my one mind, into one truth. It's not
A mere doctrine, but a union of thought
Feeling, body and mind, one field, one Earth.

Our Mother has sufficient weight and girth   790
To generate a field stronger than mine,
Older, and much more real. But what Ley line
Measures her meridian? Many do,
I think, which ancient architects well knew
At old Stonehenge. The Druids could be right
About old stones that spoke to them at night,
Aligned with stars, with sun and moon and earth
Measuring seasons, solstices, and birth
Of each New Year. We've lost their way, my son.
Their will on earth will once again be done.   800

A Third Song For Dana

So, Dana Do, a shaft of ancient sun
Light illuminated once wisdom won
By Druids in the woods with no books
To guide their thought just how a full moon looks
And stars. Our tomes contain no such wisdom
Though they're digitized here in Hell's kingdom.
Wizards once walked on earth: some were pagan
While some wore sandals; men called them Christian.

Those days are dead. The soul has shrunk, dried up
No waters flow brim flood over man's cup   810
Any longer. Models of mind are dead
That chant man's mind's contained inside the head
And brain. The world works not that way, I claim,
But this: magnetic flux follows the same
Law as spirit, a Law of God's making.

Bright Satan stomps man's foundation shaking
Thereby, old Titans, Norse gods or else Frost
Giants, mythologies modern man lost
I've found, rebirthing them from dust. Dana,
From destruction come new forms of Hannah   820
God's bread, His life and grace. Man's mind extends
Beyond his brain, the brain the mind it mends
In trauma therapy. Those arrows go
Both up and down in my model and so
Mind controls brain, grows it, heals it, drives it.
Experience has made my mind posit

Such facts. I'll test them in my lab. Say, look
Here, there. I'll log your eyebeam in my book.

My mind device will make that work, my vice
(I'll replicate my findings once, no twice,   830
No fifty times) that captures mind, holds it
In digital form. The data won't fit
Materialistic models of mind
That squeeze life, spirit, God from human kind.

My published poems tell tales like that, The Snow
Runner, Dana, can, The World Of Pan Flow
Ing does too like birds fly in high wind, cloud
Fly free then swoop, glide, fall that are allowed
By God to fly man's mind can too can soar
Drop dead or rise on an updraft of yore   840
Of good vintage. I felt one day a force
On my solar plexus, lo, a chorus
From the future, I heard, felt an event
Before it came and then I rode I went
To Hither Green where the train crashed. The dead
Called out in grief that day not to my head
But to my mind before I rode the train
That told me men have not mapped out the brain
Or its domain in full, Dana. Such things
I know no modern scientist now sings   850
But I do now commit my mind to such
Music to Keplerian spheres and much
More dreamt not by man now, here, in this place
This burial ground of our God and race.

One day in wood and field a wild rabbit
I watched crouched and waited not from habit
Brain chemical or gene but for a joke
Then ran twenty yards to prank a brown bloke
Who stood there a male pheasant who then
Hopped when rabbit ran across a small glen   860
And under his feathered tail in the air
He hopped and rabbit ran away, no care
Troubling his quick rabbit spirit. That told
Me mind exists outside man's brain an old
Knowledge, old gods that can be touched again
On Mother Earth our ancestors walked, men
Who were rooted, old trees, old truths, water
For thirsty souls, merriment and laughter
Under sleep where all our deep waters meet
As Eliot said where rest our souls and feet.   870

Eliot erred as Leavis said well. He made
Peasants foot-clogged with dull clay and he played
No pagan song. His earth was dry, cracked, no
Spring from it flowed or spirit sprung although
He felt his thirst I grant him that. Great Blake
Burned bright: his night tiger's eye can well make
Blake's God be felt in Hell here as on high.
Blake walked both worlds, honored both Earth and Sky.

Eliot's death song's a sign from God by him
Writ down pointing out the wrong path. By Him   880
Confined to death, by His hard road, His route
Away from Earth, his genius then is moot.

It records death only. I thank his mind
For that, that small sacred space that I find
In Eliot's work. Sedona rock has more.
I build my church on it thereby my floor
Is sound cosmic a vibration of God
By magnetometer told not a flawed
Tale of one mind but fact. A spirit flows
Forth, spills from rock and in round circles goes   890
Around a field from it sent forth that sings
Itself is life and is spirit. These things
I tell to thee, Dana. Here mark my word –
I'll build a science that will be read, heard
By man. The eyebeam is its crucial test.
Good normal science will reveal the rest.

A paranormal scientific shift
Comes first then I can complete Colin's gift
To modern man. The New Age kooks will dance
When man receives these data, the advance   900
Of truth on his dry earth: a new union
Of microscope and God, a completion
Of one cycle, my life. Then the healers,
Aura readers, yogis, modern feelers
Of sick chakras will have their proof. A scan
Will track the healing touch of ancient man.

Star Trek is right. We now require a gauge
In our brave world to bring down the new age
And its prana. The Legoland model
Of mechanistic mind I won't coddle.   910
A lock and key, protein-based diagram,
Newtonian nineteenth century scam

I call such thought. That mind can fit that space
Those three dimensions, it is a disgrace
When men say that. The problem can't be solved
With such equations. Is mankind not evolved?

Legoland mechanics must be broken
So quantum mind models can be spoken
Of, now and not later. That memory
Can be located, as says man's theory,   920
In three-dimensional space makes no sense
No rhyme or reason. Old primitive tents
Held better thought than that. I ask, hey, man,
Is that the best you've got? Mere maidens can
I think think thud shudder cough splutter die
Your engine will that runs your brain. And why,
You ask? Because biology has mere
Mechanism, dead mind in mind. I'm clear
On that. Lo, that dead end is dead. My head
And heart chakras long talked and then they led   930
Me far from man to Norman Wells, to Bath,
To Jessica Lake. On that sacred path
I walked long moons, long years, lost in my thought
Seeking the ancient well old Druids sought
That Holy Grail that fount or else that font
Fixed on a Ley line confluence. Men want
Cold clear water and a true church. My rock
Is rock is Earth is Sky. The dead can talk
In my science, the stars, the wind, an old
Language, knowledge and creed. The dead have told   940
Their dark secret to me my ear my rhyme
Scheme speaks it now, here, Dana, in this time
But not of time. Timeless but born in time

Bred from the Earth from dirt and dust in rhyme
Then set in a motion an emotion
An energy field that fuels a notion
A thought, a mind, and a modern vision
Of life of death and of a one nation
Called man. I need divided man to die
His truth is death is toxic and a lie.   950

Your brother walks the earth, Dana, his feet
Making many steps to get cancer beat
From sea to sea a great work and great task.
What more from his children could Colin ask?

Each one, of five, has given more to him
Than he to them, starting out first with Sim
Then you, doctor of mind and soul, student
Of neuroplasticity that God lent
To man for his healing. The mind can heal
The brain and what we think and know and feel   960
Has a field strength, an amplitude that you
Will soon study to show the world what's new
In your fine field of thought, your mind. M.D.
They'll call you soon when you set your soul free
At graduation from med school. No fool
From that peak falls to find, fails the gene pool
Lost in psychotic breaks of thought splinter
Psyche psychosis sealed though some winter
They could or have I think I know meaning
Mine of my mind though what it is seeming   970
Let me not there be lost or you. I've met
Such souls who failed to find to earn to get

God's grace, His peace, His dopamine balance
In my colleagues' professional parlance.

Do not forget the sick. Dana, they need
Your brain so their burning brains can be freed
Of their disease, souls too. In the clinic
You can make physics strengthen your physic
With scans and neural growth factor, with tools
I did not have in my career. My schools   980
Lacked that, third millennium medicine.
Our age knew not of Thomas Edison.

We chopped wood, we hauled water, and milked cows
Before class and we froze at night. The hows,
Whats, wheres and whys of things we knew not then:
Such information was not in our ken.
Antiquated we were, bent, old, near death
Barely able to breathe, to make our breath
Be seen on a cold day. A marathon
I ran it's true but that was then. I've gone   990
From bad to worse, lost teeth, my knees are stiff
My rhyming's lost its spring and my mind's stiff -
Which makes me rhyme real bad, Dana. My God
That it should come to this! Why soon a sod
Will cover me, a drunkard will I swear
And my wet grave will be my winter lair.

Oh, carry me to sea a Viking dirge
Playing fire burning but a dark night urge
Stirring. My news is good. My DNA
Survives in you. Make it live, Dana, eh.   1000

Notes

Readers may not be familiar with some of references and allusions in *Songs For Two Children*, so I have provided notes to explain content that may be obscure. Other aspects of the poem are explained in the Introduction.

Line	Note
5	No pain no gain – a motto of body builders.
20	Reference to Hiroshima, Nagasaki and the Manhattan Project.
47	Typical themes of nineteenth century English Romantic poetry.
54	Echo of Hopkins' poem, *God's Grandeur*.
59	Echo of T.S. Eliot's *Four Quartets*.
87	In his novel, *Darkness At Noon*, Arthur Koestler refers to the Communists as Neanderthals.
96	Norman Wells is where I lived in the Northwest Territories, Canada from 1970 to 1974. I also spent the summers there in 1975 to 1977. See my books, *Portrait Of Norman Wells* and *Spirit Power Drawings*.
122	Echoes of John Donne's, *Devotions Upon Emergent Occasions*, in which he writes, 'never send to know for whom the bell tolls; it tolls for thee.'
142	Jessica Lake is in the Whiteshell Provincial Park in Eastern Manitoba, Canada. I spent a lot of time there as a child. A future book is a collection of photographs I have taken there. Canyon Creek empties into the MacKenzie River south of Norman Wells.
215	The MCAT is the Medical Colleges Admission Test, which is taken when applying to medical school.
235	The anonymous medieval poem, *Corpus Christi*, is one of my favorite poems. In it, Jesus is pictured as a wounded knight lying on a stone altar.
268	The great astronomer Johannes Kepler created a celestial system in which the planets played music based on the mathematics of their positions and orbits. He was both a scientist and a mystic – we have retained his science and forgotten his mysticism.

Line	Note

275   The French philosopher, Rene Descartes, wrote his book, *Discourse On Method*, in 1637. In it he declared a complete separation of body and mind, the physical and the spiritual. This doctrine is referred to as Cartesian dualism and it is the philosophical foundation of western civilization. Contemporary science rejects the reality of the spiritual and deals only with the physical. This approach requires an assumption that the physical and spiritual are separate things; it requires dualism, with half of the duality rejected. A scientist cannot reject the spiritual if it is indistinguishable from the physical – if it is, then there must be a physics of the spirit.

297   An EEG or electroencephalogram measures brain waves.

301   The neural plexes in the body are also called ganglia. The celiac plexus is commonly called the solar plexus. The ganglia are collections of nerves in the peripheral nervous system, and are depicted in anatomy texts. They correspond to the chakras.

335   The D. H. Lawrence books relevant to these lines are *Fantasia of the Unconscious* and *Psychoanalysis and the Unconscious*.

352   Sedona, Arizona is a highly spiritual place because of its red rock formations.

424   See the drawing entitled, "Woman Pouring Tea On the Ground" in my book *Spirit Power Drawings* (2004). The woman is Cecelia Tourangeau, my former mother-in-law.

480   The Druids would often paint their faces blue before major battles and would dance on hillsides above the combat before and during the engagement.

652   I discussed a series of four books by Jeffrey Russell entitled *Satan, Lucifer, The Devil,* and *Mephistopheles* in my book *Satanic Ritual Abuse: Principles of Treatment* (1995).

Line	Note

In his books, Russell describes how the medieval, bat-winged Satan was culturally transformed into Faust, Falstaff, St. Nicholas and other characters. This process of transformation began in medieval morality plays. One variant of St. Nick not mentioned by Russell is Black Peter, a form of Santa Claus who took bad children away to Hell in a sack at Christmas time. The themes of evil, Satan, Caesar's bounty, St. Nick, and the rewarding and punishment of good and bad children have been interwoven and transformed repeatedly in the last 800 years.

704   *The Body Electric* (1985) by Robert Becker, M.D. provides background and foundation for a science of human energy fields. Becker studied the electromagnetic properties of biological organisms and was interested in the interaction between the earth's magnetic field and the human magnetic field. He demonstrated nodes of positive electrical potential corresponding to major nerve ganglia (the anatomical location of chakras) in the salamander and also demonstrated electrical correlates of chi meridians in humans. He was shunned, blackballed and shut down by the establishment, even though he published in leading scientific journals.

719   The English philosopher, John Locke, devised a mechanistic theory of visual perception in which the eye is a passive recipient of information flowing into it. This Lockean theory is adhered to by modern physiologists and perceptual psychologists, who regard the human eyebeam (called *extravision* in the psychology literature) as a superstitious fiction. They cannot investigate the possibility that the universal human experience of extravision is based on physiological reality because their theory will not allow it to be real. Demonstrating the physiological reality of the eyebeam would be a crucial confirmation of my theory of human energy fields. See my book, *Spirit Power Drawings* (2004).

Line	Note

792   Ley lines are lines of geomagnetic force on or just under the earth's surface. They intersect at culturally key locations like Stonehenge and major churches and monuments. The existence of Ley lines has not been proven with rigorous science, but has been demonstrated by dousing and other "fringe" techniques. The reality of Ley lines could be investigated with magnetometers and instrumentation used in geophysics, geology, oil, gas and mineral exploration, and related fields.

822   In my books *The Trauma Model* (2000) and *Schizophrenia* (2004) I propose that Trauma Model Therapy initiates a process of brain self-repair. For several reasons, I propose that the repair takes place mainly in a part of the brain called the hippocampus. This hypothesis can be tested by measuring the volume and function of the hippocampus with MRI and PET scans at the beginning and at the end of psychotherapy. Brain self-repair through psychotherapy will be demonstrated most robustly in people with dissociative identity disorder (more commonly known as multiple personality disorder). If this hypothesis is proven through well-designed psychotherapy studies, it will refute both mechanistic materialism and Cartesian dualism.

845   In November, 1967 I was in a train derailment at Hither Green, south of London, England in which 49 people died. I climbed out over corpses then through a hole in the roof of the train to get out; the train had come to rest lying on its side. A poem about the derailment is included in my book, *Adenocarcinoma And Other Poems*.

869   Echoes of two T.S. Eliot poems – *Marina* and *Burnt Norton*.

Two Poems
Written In 1970

I include the following two poems I wrote in 1970 to show that
I have been thinking about the themes in Songs For Two Chil-
dren for over thirty years.

The Tree
Of Life

Having rounded out that philosophy
Plotinus had no choice but to make the world fiction
And claim the world the work and not the man.
He tailored and wore the habit of words denied,
Cut, severed, chopped from their living limbs
To whirl like leaves in the rage of some man's thought.
The whole hypothesis hinged on the advent of thought
When some Greek stood up and left the assembly
And built a wall and established a limit to the law;
Rather let me attack it from this angle,
That the mind of man stood up and saw itself
But that what it saw was not mind but mirror
For truly mind is not mirrored by the world
But the world appeared mirrored by the mind
Whereas truly mind is world and mirror mirror
And the two worlds mirror the twoness of man,
Man separated from himself by seeing himself
As a reflection in the mirror of his mind
Where all images are images and not things of fact.
Thus the mind blossomed out into two thousand years
That left it without body or speech or thought
Perceiving not the world about which it argued
But some thesis or plan or red tape or empty drawer
Containing one newspaper, two combs, and a railway ticket.

The Ants and the Grasshopper

After the good training of the lamplight
No more women feared the touch of night
That made close contact with skin and lip
While the lover's moustache moved in rhythm
Not with the stars or sun or moon or the king
But the dealt hand no odds could now change;
That love game I'd like to play now my soul
Like the grasshopper that laughed at consequences.

Professorial mind formed by the student mind
Cannot displace the universal commitment;
Professors turn back eventually to taps, electricity,
The use of the car, the perpetuation and sustenance
Of the mechanical sentient and underlying principle;
The problem in the living mind is a living problem.
Outside in the organic self the rocks, trees, old Indians,
The sky, the world, the next world, the moon and death.

THE AUTHOR